Fido Says, "SIT...STAY.

...It works when humans say it!

Sandy Sutherland

Combray House

Copyright © 2024 Sandy Sutherland

All rights reserved. No part of this publication may be reproduced, stored in a retrieval system, or transmitted, in any form or by any means, electronic, mechanical, photocopying, recording, or otherwise, without the prior written permission of the author.

"Fido's Wisdom" and "What Fido Can and Can't Do" were previously published in Las Vegas Pet Scene Magazine.

Cover design by Mike Pipes.

Photos: pp. 3, 17, 36, 40, 42, 44, 46, 48, 63 67, 69, 75 & 77, by the author; p. 21, Sutherland Furniture

Sketches: pp. 13, 27, 35 & 58, Mike Pipes

Artwork: p. 4, Jane Athey

Further information: Combray House Books LLC, P.O. Box 783, Amherst MA 01004.

ISBN 978-1-958659-13-7

Contents

PART ONE 1
    About Fido 3
    Meet Fido 4

PART TWO 5
    Fido's Wisdom 7
    What Fido Can and Can't Do 9

PART THREE 11
    Fido's Lord's Prayer 13
    What Am I Here For? 15
    What I Like to Eat 17
    I want to be a Dog Someday 19
    Sitting on a Park Bench 21

PART FOUR 23
    Fido, The New Father of Twins 25
    Fido Goes Shopping 27

PART FIVE 29
    Growing up with Finley 31
    Buddy & Bailey 33
    Bella 35
    Sophie 36

    The Passing of Scooby Do 38

    Pickles 40

    Poem from Ilina 42

    What Tucker Says to the Bullies 44

    Thank you, Dr. Shim 46

    Lola the Acrobat 48

PART SIX 51

    Fido's 28th Birthday (4 human years) 53

    Fido's 35th Birthday (5 human years) 54

    Fido's 42nd Birthday (6 human years) 56

    Fido's 49th Birthday (7 human years) 58

    Fido's 56th Birthday (8 human years) 59

    Fido's 63rd Birthday (9 human years) 61

    Don't Call Me Old 63

PART SEVEN 65

    Fido Says, "Goodbye" 67

    Fido's Journey 69

PART EIGHT 73

    What Fido Meant to Us 75

Acknowledgment 77

PART ONE

About Fido

When Fido "spoke,"
Many listened.
He hopes you can hear
Some of his wisdom!

Meet Fido

My name is Fido
And when I say "Sit...Stay,"
Many of my followers,
Listen to what I say!

I might be just a dog
Some think me a little dense,
But let me make it perfectly clear,
I have a lot of common sense!

The world today is scary
For both humans and us dogs,
It seems we're run by that internet,
And all those daily blogs.

I live each day to the fullest
With my tail waggin' and flappin',
Not wishing for the UTOPIAN dream,
Just working to make it happen!

PART TWO

PART TWO

Fido's Wisdom

(My First Publication)

My friends all call me Fido
It's a common doggie name,
But after you read my poems,
You'll see I'm not the same!

Let's start with my parents
Sandy and Tony Pipes,
They chose me for their very own,
Over dogs of many types.

They feed me twice a day
It's always really good food,
This keeps me slim and healthy,
And contributes to my good mood!

They know the kind of toys I like
And keep me well supplied,
These are most appreciated,
When I'm told to stay inside.

The most important gift
I've saved to the last,
They give me so much love,
A very easy task!

What Fido Can and Can't Do

(My Second Publication)

Because I'm just a dog
There are things that I CAN'T do,
Like washing dirty dishes,
Or tying my own shoes.

But when somebody needs me
I'm Johnny on the spot,
I only ask for love in return,
That's really not a lot!

Here are some examples
Of things that I CAN do:
You can always count on me,
If you're sick or blue!

IF YOUR SICK...

I'll lay beside your bed each night
And snuggle you with my nose,
You'll feel my healing presence,
From your head to your toes!

IF YOU'RE BLUE...

I'll roll around before you
And play with my favorite toy,
You'll find me so entertaining,
Your sadness will turn to joy!

IF YOU'RE BORED...

When you're sitting at your desk
Wishing to be outside,
Know that when your work is done,
We'll be playing side by side.

IF YOUR HAPPY...

This is when I do my best
Watching your happy face,
The two of us can rule the world,
No one can take our place!

PART THREE

Fido's Lord's Prayer

Our Father who art in heaven
Thank you for the following:
My food, my bed, my mom, my dad,
And toys to keep me from wallowing!

I sleep beside their heads each night
And try to stay very quiet,
This makes me feel safe and sound,
Every dog should try it!

And when I wake, I stretch my legs
I can't wait to give them a kiss,
But morning breath sometimes makes,
This experience less than bliss!

But mom and dad don't seem to mind
They let me kiss their face,
Then I know it's breakfast time,
And to the kitchen I will race!

After that, I get a walk
To do some doggie business,
They don't let me back inside,
Without a close eyewitness!

So, thank you Lord
For all these blessings,
Without each one,
Life could be distressing!

What Am I Here For?

As a **four-legged human**
Living close to the ground,
I hear many questions,
That I think are quite profound!

The one I hear most...
"What am I here for,
Just to exist,
Or can I do more?"

This serious question
People contemplate,
But a simple answer
They don't anticipate!

Because I'm **Fido**
I can answer that,
Sit back relax,
Let's have a chat.

I live each day
Like there's no tomorrow,
This clears the way,
For less pain and sorrow.

But when pain comes
I Don't push it away,
It's a learning experience,
For a better day.

Live like me
And you'll understand,
Just being around,
Lends a helping hand.

You don't need words
To explain why you're here,
Just be a good "dog,"
You'll have nothing to fear.

What I Like to Eat

The time has come
For me to explain,
What I like to eat,
And I NEVER complain!

You see my taste
Is very diverse,
That's usually a plus,
But can be a curse!

A plus for the chef
When I chomp and I lick,
A curse when I eat something,
That makes me sick!

When I'm on my own
And walking the street,
I find lots of goodies,
On which to eat.

Let's take the flower
On the side of the road,
That looks tasty,
When in eating mode.

But flowers can be
A little tricky,
If you're NOT a dog,
That's very picky.

That's not me
I'd like to say,
Give me a bouquet,
On any ole day!

I Want to be a Dog Someday

I've often heard
My mother say,
"I want to be,
A dog someday!"

Others express
This very same thing,
Because they know,
The joy we bring!

The reason for this
Is very clear,
We believe in life,
And have no fear!

We rise in the morning
Always grateful for food,
We can easily ignore,
Any complaint or bad mood!

Unlike humans
We CAN'T be ignored,
Even if you're sick,
Or just slightly bored!

We look at you
With our big round eyes,
We get what we want,
That's no surprise.

Living like a dog
Is good for the soul,
I encourage everyone,
To strive for this goal!

Sitting on a Park Bench
(Written by Fido)

When does a human
Look a lot like me?
He might be in the park,
Contemplating a tree!

I don't see him frantically
Typing on his phone,
But he looks very peaceful,
Just sitting there alone!

I might not see him licking
A perfect stranger's hand,
But that's a BIG difference,
I completely understand.

It's actually pretty funny
The way I am linking,
This human's quiet thoughts,
To my way of thinking.

But you do the same
To me all the time,
You know I need out,
When I look at you & whine.

You might be a dog
A human or a bird,
All can "talk" with silence,
Not needing to be heard.

PART FOUR

PART FOUR

Fido, The New Father of Twins
(Author's Finley & Faith)

The first of the two
Was abruptly kicked out,
"Don't do that,"
Finley said with a shout!

It was a long 2 months
For both of them,
"Alone at last,"
Finley said with a grin!

But 10 minutes later
Faith flopped out,
"I'm back again,
And please don't pout!"

Now their living
A doggie's dream,
Adopted by humans,
To complete a team.

Now Finley and Faith
Have a new Mom and Dad,
But leaving Fido behind,
Would be incredibly sad!

So, this new team of five
Will stick together,
Through thick and thin,
And all kinds of weather!

Fido Goes Shopping
(For Finley and Faith)

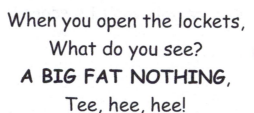

When I saw these items,
Finley & Faith came to mind,
Collars with lockets,
Such a great find!

When you open the lockets,
What do you see?
A BIG FAT NOTHING,
Tee, hee, hee!

The lockets are filled
With nothing but air,
They're way too small,
For anything to share.

The air is a symbol
Of the love that I'm sending,
It will always be available,
And never needs tending!

But if you get lost
I'll be right there,
To take you home,
Where you won't be scared!

PART FIVE

Growing up with Finley
(Written by his sister, Faith)

Finley's a hard act to follow
Day after day,
But I didn't stop trying,
That's not my way!

He could sit, he could stay
He could play with the ball,
But don't stop me there,
That's not all!

He liked to show-off
In front of his friends,
He'd rollover, or shake hands,
And get lots of grins!

There were many hard things
Finley accomplished with ease,
As his bratty little sister,
I just wanted to please!

One thing in particular
I like to shout out,
He's a loving companion,
There is no doubt!

Buddy & Bailey
(Finley and Faith's Good Friends)

They were very young
When we met these two,
And from that point on,
Our friendship grew!

But we're a lot older
Does that seem unusual?
Apparently not,
The attraction was mutual!

We wrestled and chased
In our very first meeting,
We played so hard,
There was no time for eating!

We love them so much
It's hard to explain,
The urge to tear-up,
We must constrain!

Now, they've moved on
To enjoy a new life,
Entertaining others,
And doing what's right!

Bella
(Introduced to Finley and Faith by Buddy and Bailey)

She's one of kind
You'd be tempted to PAY,
To see that face,
Throughout your day!

We tell her it's fun
To be with her,
She warms our hearts,
With her demure!!

We don't even mind
When she plays with others,
But we'd keep her to ourselves,
If we had our druthers!

That's our friend Bella
In a nutshell,
We think the world of her,
As you can probably tell!

Sophie
(Finley and Faith's Cousin)

I own the world
I could have this whole bed,
But I chose to share it,
With Uncle Tony instead!

The only problem is
He's invited two more,
If He's not more careful,
He'll be sleeping on the floor!

But Finley & Faith...
I've decided can stay,
As long as they **DON'T**,
Get in the way!

I know I am sounding
Really tough,
But in reality,
It's just a bluff!

On my daily walks
I speak to everyone,
They can see immediately,
I'm having lots of fun!

It shows in my demeanor
As I prance through the streets,
I have a wonderful life,
It can't be beat!

The Passing of Scooby-Do
(Finley and Faith's Good Friend)

We called our friend
Mr. Scooby Do,
That silly nickname,
He never outgrew!

We shared a bond
That kept us together,
Strong as an ox,
Yet light as a feather!

His two-legged mom
That he left behind,
Took great care of him,
And was always so kind!

They shared so much
As they worked and played,
His mom has memories,
That will never fade.

So, rest in peace
Dear Scooby Do,
And keep your eyes peeled,
For when we join you!

Pickles
(Written by Faith)

Finley and I loved
The cat next door,
We would romp and stomp,
And play tug-of-war!

A shy little cat,
Whose name was Pickles,
Her life was filled,
With Waggles and Wiggles!

If Finley or I
Got sick eating goo,
Pickles would know,
Exactly what to do.

You'd almost believe
She had doctor's skills,
And she'd do that magic,
Without any pills.

She always thought of others
And never herself,
Sadly, this neglect,
Would lead to bad health.

We watched with love
As they put her to sleep,
And her little heart stopped,
While she was counting sheep.

Poem from Ilina (Finley and Faith's good friend)

My name is Ilina
I'm getting pretty old,
The next step is heaven,
So I have been told!

But before I go
I'd like to say,
"I'm not afraid,
Of Judgement Day!"

My mom and dad
Have raised me well,
For that reason alone,
I won't go to hell!

I love them so much
It's hard to go,
But I'll see them again,
And that I know!

I'm still around now
Don't write me off yet,
There's a lot more to do,
With me as your pet!

What Tucker Says to the Bullies...

I don't mean to brag
But look at me,
A cute little dog,
Is what most people see!

You might have noticed,
My underbite,
Those bullying dogs,
Take quite a delight!

They can laugh and joke
And make fun of me,
But my courage is what,
Will set me free!

I'll always feel handsome
Both inside and out,
That is my strength,
There is no doubt.

I say to the bullies
"Have your fun,
Cuz you're the losers,
Once you're done!"

Thank You, Dr. Shim, (I'm Doing My Part)

Here's a subject
Close to my heart,
But actually closer,
To another body part!

From biology class,
You might recall,
They're between my legs,
And rhyme with SMALL

Doctor Shim explains
Why "they" should go,
Most of these reasons,
You already know.

Top of the list
It will alleviate,
The potential fear,
We'll overpopulate!

He also told me
I'm less likely to roam,
I'll be far more content,
Just to stay home.

Doctor Shim's the best
So, I won't worry.
I can only hope,
It's over in a hurry!

Lola, the Acrobat

My little feet
Are in the air,
In that position,
I accept the dare!

The DARE:

Standing like this
I will pee,
And not a drop
Will fall on me.

No one thinks
This can be done,
Proving them wrong,
Will be lots of fun!

(Someone in the past
Must have taught her,
To accomplish this task,
She needs lots of water!)

Once I've finished
Drinking all that,
I'll turn into
An Acrobat.

That's the **dare**
So here I go,
Now it's time,
To start this show.

PART SIX

Fido's 28th Birthday (4 human years)
(Written by Finley and Faith)

For "28" years
You've been here,
For all that time,
Let's give a big cheer!

You're not just here
You light up our day!
We love you dearly,
Is that, OK?

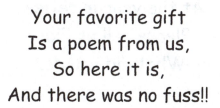

Your favorite gift
Is a poem from us,
So here it is,
And there was no fuss!!

Each and every day
You make a new friend,
This poem is an expression,
Of the love that we send!

Fido's 35th Birthday (5 human years)
(Written by Finley and Faith)

One year later
Guess what you are,
Seven years older,
Har, har, har!

Let's take a look
At the year in review,
Please tell us Fido,
What did you do?

Did you roll on the ground
And make people giggle,
Or did you turn on your back,
To get a tummy tickle?

Did you win some awards
As a late blooming poet?
If that's the case,
You didn't let us know it!

Whatever you did
We hope you had fun,
Cuz as we all know,
It can't be redone!

Fido's 42nd Birthday (6 human years)
(Written by Finley and Faith)

The past is gone
The futures not here,
That leaves only today,
To bark with no fear.

In Fido's 42 years
He's lived many todays,
But the glory of NOW,
Leaves the past in a haze!

He neither dwells in the past
Nor lives in the future,
His only goal for the day,
Is to live an adventure.

With a bone in his mouth,
And love in his heart,
He's a perfect example,
Of living life as an art!

So, thank you Fido
For being around,
To show life lived TODAY,
Makes a happy hound!!

Fido's 49th Birthday (7 human years)

Is it the 49th
Or the 50th year?
To be perfectly honest,
It's not really clear.

But, because it's Fido
It doesn't really matter,
At any age...
He just brings laughter.

We laugh when he's up
And he laughs when he's down,
He laughs with his friends,
AND when no one's around.

So Happy Birthday
To the funny "ham,"
Who brings lots of laughter,
To many a fan!

Fido's 56th Birthday (8 human years)

Please stop and think
56 is past 52,
We can only hope,
You're not slow as glue!

But we understand
You're always on the go,
So, your answer to above,
Is a clear emphatic "NO!"

Let us ask you Daddy
"What do you do each day?
Because of no new siblings,
Probably not a roll in the hay."

You might be doing less
Then you ever did before,
But let's face it, Daddy,
Pleasing humans can be a chore!

Whatever you did today
We hope it's been fun,
Leaving you eager for tomorrow,
Once this day is done!

Fido's 63rd Birthday (9 human years)
(Written by Finley and Faith)

It's hard to believe
You're 63 years old,
We can only hope,
You're not green with mold!

Finley loves you a bunch
And so does his little sister,
We both think you're more,
Then just the family jester.

You're always doing tricks
And making people laugh,
You should have been in stand-up,
But you chose a different path.

Maybe gourmet chef?
You always eat quite well,
That wasn't your choice either,
So, we won't stop and dwell!

One thing I do know
You're living the perfect life,
Giving your love to others,
And eliminating a lot of strife.

So please enjoy this day
It comes "seven" times a year,
Keep rolling over, shaking hands,
And bringing lots of cheer!

Don't Call Me Old

You can call me **older**
But never call me old,
That's what I hear,
From all the dogs I've polled.

We age much faster
Than our human counterpart,
That gives us fewer days,
To romp, play and bark!

So watch us close
But let us play,
To our hearts content,
Till our dying day.

PART SEVEN

PART SEVEN

Fido Says, "Goodbye!"

I haven't been feeling
My tiptop best,
So I went to the doctor,
To have some tests!

When the X-ray showed
A big round blob,
That's when my kids,
Began to sob!

With a tear in their eye,
But a smile on their face,
They talked to me about,
A better place!

They told me they'd always
Be with me in spirit,
But the simple truth was,
I didn't want to hear it!

But the more they talked
The better it sounded,
There'll be no more chaos,
Every dog's grounded!

My craving for food
And toys will cease,
And in their place,
Will come joy and peace!

Now they're not sure
But they think there's a phone,
But even without it,
I can always call home!

Just place my paw
Over my heart,
Call their names,
And our exchange will start!

So, thanks to everyone
For a wonderful life,
I'll be back to see you,
At least once or twice!

Fido's Journey...

At the doctor's office,
Once I'd said goodbye,
I started the journey,
You take when you die!

A question I asked
That sounded like a song,
"Where are we going,
And will it take long?"

I heard a voice
Both loud and clear,
"Don't think about time,
You have nothing to fear!

"From this day forward,
You'll be living like a flower,
Not knowing or caring,
What is the hour!"

And before I knew it
I was standing there,
At the Pearly Gates,
A sight so rare!

The faces I saw
Looking back at me,
Were friends I'd lost early,
And dear family!

I heard them whisper
In St Peter's ear,
"Please let him in,
Fido's a dear!"

But now is the time
For His decision,
Will I go up or down,
That is the question!

All of a sudden
The gates opened wide,
And the trapdoor below me,
Was sealed up tight!

The next thing I knew
My tumor was gone,
And in its place,
A brand-new dawn!

Now...this granite statue
Watches over me
And protects the life
That has been set free.

PART EIGHT

PART EIGHT

What Fido Meant to Us!

Our Dad, Fido
Was a doctor of sorts,
He brough a clear reality,
To all that life distorts!

A four-legged human
That gave all his love,
To those that he found special,
And the Man above!

His daily doggie life
Might have seemed a little boring,
Eating, sleeping, walking,
Even a little snoring!

Our dear furry Daddy
Was on call day and night,
The comfort he brought to all,
Was truly out of sight!!

Acknowledgment

Without the constant & loving
support from my two-legged mom, Sandy,
this book could never have happened.

She inspired me, Fido, to write!
That encouraged my family, Finley, and Faith
to follow in my **FOUR** "paw-steps!"

For those of you that don't know
I chose to change my name,
Calling me Fido, not Hugo,
Might bring me fortune & fame.

Made in the USA
Monee, IL
23 September 2024

65721315R00046